JANE ADDAMS

PEOPLE WHO MADE A DIFFERENCE

David and Patricia Armentrout

Rourke Publishing LLC
Vero Beach, Florida 32964

© 2002 Rourke Publishing LLC

PHOTO CREDITS:
Photos provided by the Jane Addams Memorial Collection, JAMC negs. 2, 4, 15, 140, 151, 556, 837, 850, 920, 1054, 1639, Special Collections, The University Library, University of Illinois at Chicago

EDITORIAL SERVICES:
Pamela Schroeder

Library of Congress Cataloging-in-Publication Data

Armentrout, David, 1962-
    Jane Addams / David & Patricia Armentrout.
        p. cm. -- (People who made a difference)
Includes index.
ISBN 1-58952-054-8
 1. Addams, Jane, 1860-1935--Juvenile literature. 2. Women social workers--United States--Biography--Juvenile literature. 3. Women social reformers--United States--Biography--Juvenile literature. [1. Addams, jane, 1860-1935. 2. Social Workers. 3. Women--Biography. 4. Nobel Prizes--Biography.] I. Armentrout, Patricia, 1960-II. Title.

HV28.A35 A75 2001
361.92--dc21
[B]   2001018582

Printed in the USA

TABLE OF CONTENTS

Who was Jane Addams?   5

Jane's Childhood   6

Jane and her Father   9

Learning About Poverty   11

Jane's Education   12

Jane's Plan for Hull House   17

Nobel Peace Prize   20

Important Dates to Remember   22

Glossary   23

Index   24

Further Reading/Websites to Visit   24

WHO WAS JANE ADDAMS?

Jane Addams helped children and the poor. She fought for equal rights and for world peace.

Jane and her friend Ellen Starr opened a **settlement house** in Chicago. The house was a friendly and safe place for **immigrants** and their children.

Jane Addams won the **Nobel Peace Prize** in 1931.

Jane Addams was the first American woman to receive the Nobel Peace Prize.

JANE'S CHILDHOOD

Jane was born in Cedarville, Illinois, in 1860. Her father, John Huy Addams, was a **senator** and owned a mill. Jane's mother Sara died when Jane was just two. John Addams remarried. Jane's stepmother was Anna Haldeman, who had two children of her own.

Jane Addams at age eight

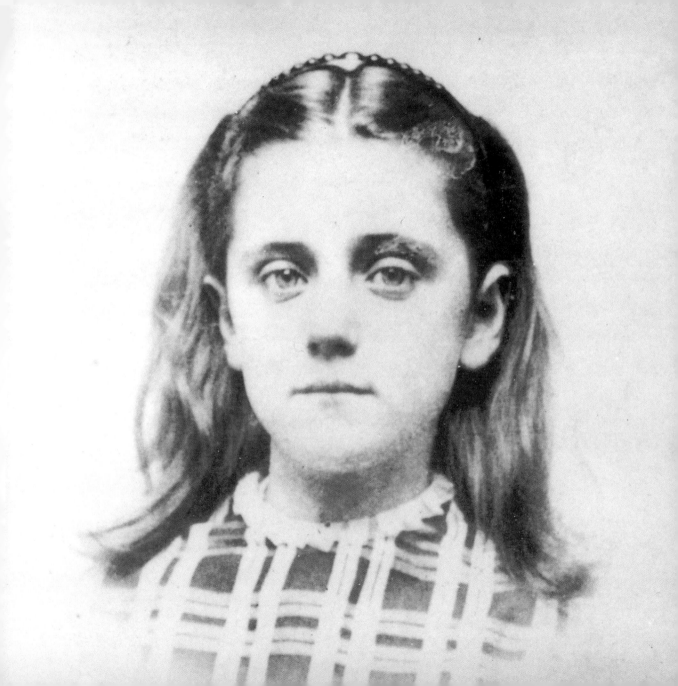

JANE AND HER FATHER

Jane loved spending time with her father. She watched him when he taught his Bible class. She liked to be around him and other adults.

John Addams was smart and successful. He was a fair man, too. John Addams did not believe in slavery. He secretly helped slaves who came through the **Underground Railroad**.

Jane's family home in Cedarville, Illinois

LEARNING ABOUT POVERTY

Jane was used to having everything she needed. She lived in a big house with a loving family. One day Jane went on a trip with her father. Jane saw people living in small, run-down homes. She wondered why people lived that way. Jane's father said that some people had no choice but to live in **poverty**.

Seeing these run-down houses made Jane Addams sad.

JANE'S EDUCATION

When Jane reached her teens she went to the Rockford Female Seminary. She graduated with high grades. She dreamed of going to medical school.

During the summer of 1881 Jane's father became ill and died. Jane felt very alone without her father. She didn't know what to do with her life. Jane finally decided to work in medicine.

Jane with her stepmother and stepbrother after her father's death

Jane went to the Women's Medical College of Philadelphia. After her first year she began to have back pain. Jane was born with a curved spine and it started to affect her health. She had surgery to help her, but had to drop out of medical school to get better.

In 1883, Jane traveled in Europe. She enjoyed the beautiful and interesting places she visited. Jane, however, was unhappy about the poor people she saw there.

14

Ellen Starr was Jane's good friend. She later helped Jane open Hull House.

JANE'S PLAN FOR HULL HOUSE

Jane spent the next few years learning about ways to help the poor. She visited Toynbee Hall in London. There, she saw workers in a poor part of town helping the needy. Jane thought the hall was a great idea.

Jane talked to her friend Ellen Starr about her plan to help the needy. Ellen agreed to help Jane and the two women met in Chicago.

*Jane and Ellen opened
Hull House in 1889.*

Jane and Ellen rented a house in the Chicago **slums**. They called the house Hull House.

Jane and Ellen used their own money and furniture. They took money people gave them and made the house beautiful.

Hull House opened in 1889 as a settlement house—a place for the needy. It was a success. Jane was living up to her dreams of helping others.

A family is greeted at the door of Hull House in Chicago.

NOBEL PEACE PRIZE

Jane Addams helped the poor. However, she also fought for equal rights, clean work places, and world peace. She wrote books and made many speeches in her lifetime.

In 1931 Jane Addams won the Nobel Peace Prize. Her lifelong work was honored around the world.

Jane visited and helped people at Hull House up to her death in 1935.

Jane Addams greets children at the Mary Crane Nursery at Hull House.

IMPORTANT DATES TO REMEMBER

1860	Born in Cedarville, Illinois (September 6)
1877	Began school at the Rockford Female Seminary
1881	Death of John Huy Addams
1883	Traveled in Europe
1889	Opened Hull House
1931	Won Nobel Peace Prize
1935	Died in Chicago (May 21)

GLOSSARY

immigrants (IM ih grents) — people who move to a new country to live

Nobel Peace Prize (noh BEL PEES PRYZ) — a prize of money awarded each year to someone who helps people around the world

poverty (PAHV er tee) — having very little money; poor

senator (SEN et er) — a member of the senate; a law-maker

settlement house (SET el ment HOWS) — a house in a poor area of town with nice things and services for the poor like babysitting, meeting rooms, a gymnasium, and a library

Underground Railroad (UN der grownd RAYL rohd) — a secret organization during the early 1800s that helped slaves escape to northern states

slums (SLUMZ) — an overcrowded poor area of town with run-down houses

INDEX

Addams, John Huy   6, 9
Addams, Sara   6
Haldeman, Anna   6
Hull House   17, 18, 20
immigrants   5
Nobel Peace Prize   5, 20

Rockford Female Seminary   12
settlement house   5, 18
Starr, Ellen   5, 17, 18
Toynbee Hall   17
Underground Railroad   9

Further Reading

Carman Harvey, Bonnie. *Jane Addams* Enslow Publishers, Inc. ,1999
Diliberto, Gioia. *A Useful Women* A Lisa Drew Book/Scribner, 1999

Websites To Visit

- www.lkwdpl.org/wihohio/adda-jan.htm
- www.swarthmore.edu/library/peace

About The Authors

David and Patricia Armentrout specialize in nonfiction writing. They have had several books published for primary school reading. They reside in Cincinnati, Ohio with their two children.